Department of Education and Science
Scottish Education Department
Welsh Office

Meeting Special Educational Needs

A brief guide by Mrs. Mary Warnock
to the Report of the Committee
of Enquiry into Education
of Handicapped Children and
Young People

London: Her Majesty's Stationery Office

© Crown copyright 1978
First published 1978
Tenth impression 1985

ISBN 0 11 270478 6

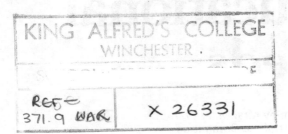

Meeting Special Educational Needs

Introduction

The Committee of Enquiry, whose full report, *Special Educational Needs*, was published in 1978, was set up in 1974. It first met in September of that year and its last meeting was in March 1978. Its terms of reference were 'to review educational provision in England, Scotland and Wales for children and young people handicapped by disabilities of body or mind, taking account of the medical aspects of their needs, together with arrangements to prepare them for entry into employment; to consider the most effective use of resources for these purposes; and to make recommendations'.

This booklet sets out the main findings of the Committee, sketches the Committee's general view of special education and explains the steps it thought needed most urgently to be taken to improve the quality of special education. For the sake of convenience English terminology (such as local education authority and social services department) is employed in this booklet, as in the full report, to avoid repetition of the corresponding Scottish terminology. No attempt is made in this booklet to take account of differences in special educational provision between England, Scotland and Wales: for example there is no provision in Scotland corresponding to Section 10 of the Education Act 1976. The main recommendations of the report and the order of priority assigned to them, however, hold equally for England, Scotland and Wales. The order of presentation differs from that of the full report: nevertheless it is hoped that the connections between the different recommendations will become apparent; for although the field covered by the Committee was vast the different areas were all linked. The concept of *special educational need*, as delineated in the report, is a unifying concept; it is not revolutionary, by any means. To some extent the Committee was analysing and clarifying ideas which were already beginning to be put into practice. But a further change of attitude will be necessary, among professionals and the general public alike, if actions are indeed to follow words. The Committee hopes that its report will contribute to such a change.

Aims and needs

The Committee of Enquiry started work only a few years after the implementation of the Education (Handicapped Children) Act 1970 (the corresponding 1974 Act in Scotland was not implemented until 1975). By these Acts all handicapped children, however severe their disability were included in the framework of special education. Henceforth no child, however great his disabilities, was regarded as ineducable. The Committee endorsed this view by stating that education is a good to which *all* children are entitled.

The Committee also held that the aims of education are the same, whatever the advantages or disadvantages of the boy or girl concerned. The aims are, first, to increase a child's knowledge of the world he lives in and his imaginative understanding, both of the possibilities of that world and of his own responsibilities in it; and, secondly, to give him as much independence and self-sufficiency as he is capable of, by teaching him those things he must know in order to find work and to manage and control his own life. Children have manifestly different obstacles to overcome in their path towards this double goal, and for some the obstacles are so enormou that the distance they travel will not be very great. But for these children any progress at all is significant. For the most severely handicapped, education seeks to help them overcome their difficulties one by one.

If the aims of education are agreed, then an *educational need* is determined in terms of whatever is essential for the attainment of these aims. Special education is the meeting of the special needs of a child in order to approach the goals. The quality of special education, moreover, can be judged according to how well it satisfies those needs. We have to ask whether a child receiving such education is, finally, appreciably nearer the twin goals of understanding and independence. In one sense educational needs are common to all children, just as educational aims are common. In another sense, each child's needs are specific to him: they are what he needs if he is, individually, to make progress. So the Committee thought of educational needs as forming roughly speaking a continuum. Any extra help which must be given to a child, either temporarily or permanently, to prevent or overcome an educational handicap, could be seen as *special educational provision*, wherever it was provided.

Wider concept of special education

The concept of special education employed by the Committee was therefore appreciably widened, as was the notion of the children who might need it. The Committee rejected the idea of two distinct groups of children, the handicapped and the non-handicapped, of whom the former had special education, while the latter just had education. On the contrary, just as needs were seen to form a continuum, so special education itself was seen as a continuum of provision, ranging from temporary help to permanent and long-term adaptation of the ordinary curriculum. The Committee therefore recommended that *the distinction between special and remedial education should be dropped*, and that the assumption should be that perhaps as many as one child in five might need special educational help at some stage during his school career. In this sense, then, special education becomes a far broader and more flexible concept.

The far-reaching implications of this widening of the concept cannot be too strongly emphasised. If up to one in five children may need special educational provision in the course of a school career, this does not imply that up to one in five are to be thought of as handicapped in the traditional sense of the term. With proper help, the educational problems of the majority will be temporary; without it they will be compounded by a continuing experience of failure. The Committee referred to any child who needed such help as *a child with a special educational need*, and it is with such needs, however long or short their duration, however severe or minor, that the report is concerned.

A special educational need may take various forms. There may be need for provision of special means of access to the curriculum, through, for example, special equipment or specialised teaching techniques; or need for a modified curriculum; or there may be need for particular attention to the social structure and emotional climate in which education is taking place.

The form of a child's need is not necessarily determined by the nature of his disability or disorder. At present children are categorised according to their disabilities and *not* according to their educational needs. But the Committee recommended that *statutory categorisation of handicapped pupils should be abolished*. The basis for decision about the type of educational provision required should be not a single label, but rather a detailed description of the special need in question. One great advantage of such a system would be that the many children who suffer from more than one of the old 'handicaps' would not now be described simply but vaguely as 'multiply handicapped'. On the contrary, provision would be made for them according to a detailed description of their complex educational need.

However, the Committe recognised that some descriptive terms were needed. For example, the wide concept of 'learning difficulty' should be used to describe both those children needing remedial help, and those at present described as 'ESN(M)' or 'ESN(S)'. One could then go on to specify that the learning difficulties were mild, moderate or severe. The term 'maladjusted' might be retained for children whose difficulties were mainly emotional or behavioural.

The Committee accordingly recommended that when a child is assessed as in need of special educational provision a detailed profile of him should be completed and that the local education authority should make decisions in the light of this information about how to meet those needs. (Assessment is discussed more fully later in this booklet, page 16).

A new system of recording need

The Committee realised that the old system of categorisation had the major advantage of safeguarding the rights of a child who fitted into one of the categories to an education suited to his needs. In order to protect the interests of children with severe, complex or long term disabilities, it recommended there should be a system of *recording as in need of special educational provision*. This recording would lay an obligation on a local education authority to make special provision for a recorded child on the basis of the profile of his needs. It would not impose a single label of handicap on the child, but would embody a positive statement of the special provision he requires. This system of recording would form an integral part of the much broader framework of special education and apply to that minority of pupils whose needs cannot be met within the resources generally available at ordinary schools. *The broad framework itself is intended to establish once for all the idea that special educational provision, wherever it is made, is additional or supplementary provision*, rather than as it used to be, quite separate or alternative.

Importance of starting early and continuing late

The Committee widened the notion of special education in another way. In the case of children who show signs of disability at birth or soon after, it argued that education must start at once. Education is not something which goes on only at school. Children with severe disabilities need to be taught things which other children would just pick up without teaching; and for most of these children their parents would be the best teachers. Teaching by parents is thus an important part of special education. Education must be thought of as including not only the education of children from five upwards, but, crucially, the education of children far below that age.

The notion of special educational need was extended too, at the other end of the age range to cover those young people with disabilities or significant difficulties who had reached or passed school-leaving age but who were still progressing towards understanding and independence. The educational content of provision for such young people from sixteen to nineteen or beyond is seen to be of the greatest importance. In many ways, the more excellent the provision for children of school age becomes, the more urgent the need to continue this provision after the age of sixteen has been reached, when learning might just be beginning to get faster and more productive. In this area, too, the concept of special education is extended.

It was at these two ends of the age range that the Committee placed its first priorities. Although all the recommendations of the report were held to be important, it was thought necessary, in a time of financial restriction, to argue that some of the recommendations should be implemented first. And it was in the field of the education of children under five and of young people over sixteen that the present state of special education seemed least satisfactory.

The very young

The successful education of very young children requires a close and, wherever possible, equal relationship between parents and professionals – not only teachers but doctors and sometimes social workers. Many severe congenital abnormalities in children are recognised within the first few days following birth or within the first few months. The discovery may be made by doctors or health visitors or, in many cases, the parents may be the first to detect signs of such conditions. A good deal of the evidence to the Committee indicated both that the disclosure to parents of such abnormalities is often handled badly and that parents had difficulty in convincing anyone that there was something wrong with their child. Parents need a great deal of support and a lot of time to absorb the information they are given and to ask questions. It is important that they should be told as soon as possible about available facilities and supporting services, and that they should be helped to realise that they do not have to cope with their child's problems alone.

The *educational* possibilities for children with disabilities and serious difficulties should be discussed with the parents straight away. All doctors and nurses involved at this early stage should show themselves aware of the educational implications of handicap and should know where parents may go for further information and guidance.

With a bewildering array of professionals and services, parents may be confused about where to turn for help and advice. The Committee thought it important that as soon as a child has been found to have a disability or to be showing signs of special needs and problems *one single 'named person' should be designated to provide a point of contact for the parents of that child*.
In the very early years of the child's life the 'named

person' should normally be the health visitor, who is likely to be known and trusted by the parents and to have ready access to the home. But the health visitor must be working in close cooperation with the social and other services. Links with the education service are essential to enable her to pass on information about the needs of the child to the local education authority, and to help her to appreciate the crucial importance of very early education and to guide the parents in making contact with the available services.

It is not only when their child is below school age that parents will need one single point of contact with the professionals responsible for his education. This is a continuing need. When the child begins to go to school the 'named person' would normally be the headteacher of the school; and in the case of young people over school leaving age the careers officer or the specialist careers officer should normally act as the single point of contact for the young people, and their parents, during the transition from school to adult life, or ensure that another professional takes on this function.

For parents of very young children one of the main functions of the 'named person' would be to ensure that the parents have the support and help of peripatetic teachers. Such teachers (at present widely available only for the teaching of deaf children) should concentrate on very young children and on specific disabilities as far as this is possible. *Without a substantial increase in this service many children are wasting the most crucial time for their education.* An important part of the service would be to work with parents, support them, and help them to teach their own children as well as working directly with the children themselves.

The Committee was also insistent that there should be a great increase in nursery education, not only for children with special educational needs, but for all children. Most children with special needs would then be able to start their education with other children of their own age, in an ordinary class. As this might not be practical for children with very severe or complex difficulties there should be *some* special nursery classes and units as well.

It was argued that opportunities should be widely available in playgroups, opportunity groups and day nurseries, all of which can be of inestimable value to children with special needs and to their parents. Such groups depend upon professional support, and part of the work of peripatetic teachers should be to provide such support and expertise with the help of professionals working in the health and social services. Voluntary organisations also have a very important part to play in starting and organising playgroups, day nurseries and opportunity groups, and there must be increased cooperation between them and local authorities if the best possible service is to be provided.

The improvement of facilities for education in the very early years therefore constituted one of the priorities for the Committee. It is not clear whether local education authorities are permitted to provide education for children under two at present, nor is it certain that the term 'education' has any legal significance for children below that age. The Committee held that the law must be clarified on this point. The needs of children with special problems *involve education from birth onwards*. In the development of language, for example, a child can learn more before the age of three than at any other time in his life. Expert skilled teaching therefore needs to be available for children with major difficulties, whether through deafness or other disabilities, and parents must be helped to help their own children. No aspect of the education of handicapped children could be more important than this.

After school-leaving age

The Committee's recommendations for young people over school-leaving age were also stressed. A pupil's needs should be reassessed while he is still at school, and a full discussion undertaken of the possibilities for the individual pupil, involving all the professionals concerned, the parents, and the pupil himself, wherever feasible. Meanwhile it is the duty of all schools which have pupils with special needs to *ensure*, as far as possible, that by the time pupils leave, they have been equipped with the basic social and academic skills necessary for adult life. The needs of young people will be very varied, and corresponding provision must be made if opportunities are to be genuinely extended.

For some school leavers, further education will be the key to continued educational development. Local education authorities need to adopt a coordinated approach to the further education of young people with special needs and make available a range of provision, probably on a regional basis, and in the context of a long-term plan; they should publicise the provision made. Some colleges of further education, for example, should be prepared to experiment with modified versions of ordinary courses; some colleges should provide special vocational courses at operative level, and training in social competence and independence, in order to continue the work of the schools. Within every region there should be at least one special unit to provide further education for young people with very severe difficulties and disabilities, based in an existing establishment of further education. It should be possible for those young people who may be able to proceed to higher education, or their advisers, to discover what facilities are available for them at universities and polytechnics. The Committee recommended that higher education establishments should publicise their policy on the admission of disabled students and make systematic efforts to look after their needs, particularly their need for careers advice.

The age of sixteen may be critical in the development of young people currently described as severely educationally subnormal, who experienced severe learning difficulties while they were at school, and who, without continuing educational opportunities, may actually fall back. Some may appropriately stay at school for a further two years, but because some schools, especially if they cater for children of all ages, may not be able to provide the right conditions, it may be important for the maturity of the pupils for them to leave at sixteen.

At present some pupils stay on at school because no places are available for them at adult training centres. Some young people have to wait aimlessly at home until a place becomes available. A range of provision should be available for them when they leave school and be preeminently educational in purpose. All adult training centres and day centres should have a strong educational

9

element, and although these centres are provided by the social services departments of local authorities, the Committee considered it appropriate for *the educational element to be organised by the education service.*

If education is not provided, and taken seriously, and if highly professional teaching is not available, a valuable period in the life of these young people will be wasted. Suc education may make the crucial difference for them betwe a life of total dependence and one of reasonable freedom and purpose. Similarly, for those who need long-term hospital care the onus should be on the education authority to provide programmes of continuing education meet individual needs, and to make programmes available for those who have passed the age of sixteen.

Turning to employment, the Committee held that the publ service and the nationalised industries should review thei employment policies in order to open their doors more widely to people with disabilities and to provide more imaginative work opportunities for them. Local education authorities, through their careers services, should promot discussions with employers' and employees' organisations to try to persuade employers to take on young people with disabilities. These discussions should be held in conjunctic with the Manpower Services Commission and, where necessary, with the social services department.

Young people who will be employed in sheltered work need a progressive programme of activities designed to ensure that, if possible, they may be able to leave the sheltered environment for open employment. A wider range of work, both skilled and unskilled, should be available; and above all there should be increased provision of such workshops.

It is easy to give such provision low priority in a time of financial difficulty, but failure to provide genuine educational opportunities for young people with disabilitie at this stage of their career may lead not only to human misery and frustration but also to the need for costly support at a later stage.

Local authorities should be more generous in, for example, using their powers to make discretionary awards to young people who enter further education. Research and

experiment should take place in the provision and design
of aids for the disabled, and in the provision of different
forms of long and short-term residential accommodation.

Children of school age

These then, were the Committee's first two areas of equal
priority. But it should not be thought that between the
years of early education and those of transition from school
to adult life there are no changes to be made. Far from it,
the Committee considered that the whole range of provision
for children of school age, whether in special schools or
ordinary schools, needed to be looked at afresh.

The wide concept of special education and the conclusion
that up to one in five children are likely to require special
educational provision at some time during their school
career means that the majority of children with special
needs must be identified and also taught within the
ordinary school. A number of different forms of provision in,
or closely connected with, ordinary schools is therefore
needed. Where a child's need for special access to the
curriculum can be met through, for example, special
equipment such as a hearing aid, or ramps to classrooms, it
may be quite possible for that child to continue full-time
education in an ordinary class. Where a modified
curriculum is needed or either specialist teaching
techniques or the more intimate atmosphere of small
teaching groups, some or all of the child's education will
have to take place in a special class or other supporting
base. There must be flexibility and an openness to the
notion of adapting provision to the particular needs of
individual children.

Those needing special schools

Some children will be best educated in a special school.
There are at least three groups for whom this is likely to be
true: those with severe or complex disabilities – physical,
sensory or intellectual – who need special facilities or
teaching expertise which would be impossible or very
difficult and costly to provide in ordinary schools; those
with severe emotional or behavioural disorders who have
difficulty in forming any relationships or whose behaviour
is so extreme or unpredictable that it causes disruption in

11

an ordinary school or prevents other children from benefiting from education; and those whose disabilities m. be less severe, but often multiple, and who, despite help, d not flourish in an ordinary school.

Information about the range of provision in each area needs to be readily available both to professionals concerned with the assessment and placement of children and to parents whose children have special needs. The Department of Education and Science and Scottish Education Department should include in their lists of special schools a description of the kinds of special educational need which each residential special school caters for. More important, each local authority should produce its own handbook containing details of all special educational provision for children recorded as needing suc provision and of the particular educational needs catered for by each school.

Integration

It follows from what has so far been said that the thorny question of 'integration', 'mainstreaming' or 'normalisation' must be considered afresh. Arguments about integration have, in the past, been conducted in terms of perhaps 2 per cent of all children who, in the old sense, needed 'special educational treatment'. Since this usually meant education in a special school the debate centred on whether all children at present in special schools could or should in future be educated in ordinary schools. It was against such a background that Section 10 of the 1976 Education Act was enacted, to become operativ on a day to be appointed by the Secretary of State for Education and Science. This has the effect that, subject to certain qualifications and from the appointed date, handicapped pupils should be educated in ordinary schools rather than in special schools.

If special education is no longer defined in terms of *the place where the education is to take place*, but in terms rather of *what needs it is designed to meet:* and if about 20 per cent rather than 2 per cent of children may have some special needs at some time in their school career, it is clear that most of these needs will be met in ordinary schools. Successful provision for different needs will depend partly

1

on the resources available to the school, and partly on the attitudes and the expertise of the teachers. It will also depend on the precise interpretation of the expression 'the ordinary school'. There may well be children who are in an ordinary school but whose educational needs demand that, for at least a part of every day, they will be withdrawn from the ordinary class for special teaching, just as children are now often withdrawn for remedial teaching. For some children the special teaching may occupy most, even all, of the school day and may continue for as long as the child is at school. For others, after a relatively short time, even these brief withdrawal periods may come to an end, so that the child goes back full-time to the ordinary class. It is in the use of such special withdrawal classes, or special units, which a child may join either full-time or part-time, for long or short periods, that the imagination and flexibility of ordinary schools will be apparent. Indeed the Committee recommended that every large ordinary school should have a special resource centre or other supporting base. Integration, therefore has no one precise meaning; and the debate has often been clouded by this ambiguity, and by a lack of clarity about exactly who are the children to be integrated, and with whom.

Role of special schools

There remains a crucial task for the special schools in the whole range of educational provision for children with special needs. This is partly because there will always be some children who can be educated only in special schools. Moreover, as the numbers in special schools decline (with the falling school population, improvements in preventive medicine, and health care), there will be scope for special schools to develop increased specialisation and expertise.

The Committee envisaged that some of these schools should be *specifically developed as resource centres* for use by all teachers in a particular area. Such centres would be used for curriculum development and the in-service education of teachers. They could also be places where parents and professionals could refer for advice on special education, and where parents could meet each other. The preparation, storage and loan of specialised equipment and materials and the development of audio-visual materials would all be part of the functions of such centres.

Moreover, staff of schools would offer expert advice and support to the teachers in ordinary schools, who will have to learn how to teach children with special needs. Thus, though the number of special schools may decline their work will become increasingly central and influential.

Boarding special schools

These considerations apply as much to boarding special schools as to day schools, and specialist centres for relatively rare or particularly complex disabilities should be based in residential special schools, or schools with som residential facilities.

There will always be children whose disabilities demand a combination of medical treatment, education, therapy and care which would be beyond the resources of a day school and their parents to provide. Such children are likely to include those suffering from severe sensory loss, extensive neurological damage or malfunction, severe emotional or behavioural disorder, or severe difficulties in communication. There are also children whose learning difficulties or other barriers to progress require consistent and continuous educational influence such as can be provided only in a residential setting; and others who cannot live at home and receive the sustained attention they need without unacceptable damage to the rest of the family. Again, a poor social environment or disturbed family relationships may actually contribute to educationa difficulties and for such children, therefore, boarding school is essential.

The Committee urged that the types of school should remain varied, offering different kinds of residential accommodation (including some of a hostel type), and that more boarding special schools should be prepared to accept children, at short notice and for brief periods, whenever the need arises, for example, for intensive specialist tuition or for relief during family emergencies.

Non-maintained special schools

Some special schools are non-maintained (ie they are not maintained by local education authorities). The Committee stressed that educational standards in such schools should be as high as those in maintained special schools, and that for this reason they should be subject to much closer oversight than at present by the local education authorities who use them, and by Her Majesty's Inspectorate. Links between these schools and local education authorities are necessary and, in order to promote them, each school should have its own governing body which should include at least one representative of the appropriate local education authority.

The same considerations apply, with perhaps even greater force, to those numerous independent schools which cater wholly or mainly for handicapped pupils. A very large proportion of the children placed in these schools by local authorities are boarders; this fact in itself shows that there is a serious shortage of maintained boarding schools for children with special needs. Local education authorities taking up places in independent schools must satisfy themselves that the schools are actually providing education and health care of a standard comparable with that of their own special schools. To make this possible, both the local education authority in which a school is situated and the authority which sends pupils to the school must be offered access to the school; and, once again, each school should have a governing body which includes local authority representatives.

Community homes
Besides boarding schools, there are other residential establishments in which educational provision may be made for children with special needs: including community homes and hospitals. Some community homes, run by the social services department of local authorities, provide education on the premises. Although such education is not specifically or uniquely for children with special educational needs, it is obvious that the children who are educated there are often suffering from educational difficulties and that they have needs in common with children in special schools for the maladjusted. Teachers who work in these establishments are employed by the social services department, or in some case are seconded by the education department of the authority, with the result that they may feel isolated from the mainstream of special education, and may receive much less support and advice

from advisory teachers or other experts than do teachers in special schools.

The Committee was of the strong opinion that education in community homes should be seen as part of the regular provision of education for children with special needs and that teachers in such homes should be in the service of the local education authorities.

Hospitals

There are also children who, for short or long periods, are in hospital. The education provided is not always of a high standard, nor is it always taken as seriously as education in special schools would be. It is important that, as far as possible, the educational activities of a child in hospital, however profoundly disabled, should be distinct from the other hospital activities. Ideally there should be separate educational premises in every hospital where children stay for long periods (such as mental handicap hospitals). Again the Committee argued strongly for all hospital education to be regarded as part of the mainstream of special education, and that teachers who undertake this demanding and difficult work should be supported by the advisory services and should be able, like their colleagues in schools, to attend courses and increase their expertise through in-service training. Only in this way can the quality of hospital education be improved.

Assessment

With the abolition of categories of handicap, the concept of ascertaining a child as in need of special education according to the categories will also go, but the effective discovery and assessment of educational need will be as crucial in the future as it is now.

Once a child begins to attend a nursery class or a school it may well be a teacher who will discover signs of a handicapping condition. All teachers must be trained to be observant, and to interpret such signs as soon as possible.

Record keeping

A folder should be kept for every school child, containing

records of his progress, facts about illness, absences from school, the composition of his family, an account of work schemes followed and the results of any attainment or diagnostic tests. Such a folder would be useful for all children, especially when they transfer from one school to another. But it would be particularly useful for those who might later need special educational provision. It would go far towards ensuring early detection and effective assessment of special needs. Such a folder should be available to the child's parents, class teacher and to any personal tutor or, later, careers adviser in contact with the child. There should, where necessary, be a second and confidential folder, where there have been professional consultations about a child, containing the results of such consultations and any sensitive information given in confidence about a child's background or circumstances. Such a folder should also be kept at school, with access to it controlled by the headteacher.

Stages of assessment

Against this background of improved record-keeping the Committee proposed that there should be five stages of assessment for children at school, and that a child's needs should be assessed at one or more of these stages (though very rarely at all five) as appropriate.

Stage 1 would probably involve the class teacher or some other member of staff closely concerned who consults the head of the school about a child who is falling behind or is showing other signs of special educational need. At this first stage the head would be responsible for marshalling information about the child's performance at school, together with information from medical, social and other sources and, where possible, extra information from his parents. Then a decision would be taken about what special provision should be made available within the competence of the school.

The same procedure would take place at *Stage 2*, but the child's difficulties would then be discussed with a teacher with training and expertise in special education. The options for further action would then be the same as for Stage 1, with the additional possibility of prescribing a special programme for the child, to be supervised by the specialist or advisory teacher.

If it is decided at Stage 2 to seek further advice, or if, on further review, the child is found not to be making progress, then assessment would take place at *Stage 3* by a professional or professionals brought in by the headteacher of the school or the school doctor and with the advice of a specialist or advisory teacher. The professional might be a peripatetic teacher, such as a teacher of the deaf, an educational psychologist, or a member of the health or social services. The options at Stage 3 would be to make special arrangements at the child's school or to refer the child *for multi-professional assessment at Stages 4 or 5*. The child would move on to one of these stages only if it was thought that specialist educational provision was needed on a regular basis *external to the school*. It is only at this stage that the SE forms procedure* should be initiated by the headteacher of the school.

The multi-professional assessment beyond Stage 3 would be carried out at one or both of two stages (*Stages 4 and 5*). The stages would be distinguished from each other primarily by the degree and amount of specialist expertise involved. The professionals taking part in assessment at *Stage 4* would be those directly responsible for *local* services for children with disabilities, for example a medical officer, health visitor, educational psychologist and social worker based in the locality, a teacher in a local school and a special education advisory teacher with local responsibilities. They would be able to take decisions about the use of local facilities and resources or refer children, where necessary, for further investigation at *Stage 5*. Such a group of experts ought to be able to come together at short notice; they should be prepared to carry out their assessment in a variety of settings, more usually at school, and the headteacher of the school (or the class teacher of, for instance, the nursery class) should normally take part in the assessment.

At Stage 5 the professionals involved might be the same as

---

* This procedure is explained in DES Circular 2/75, Welsh Office Circular 21/75, *The discovery of children requiring special education and the assessment of their needs* (17 March 1975) and in the Scottish Education Department's letter of 1 November 1971.

those involved at the earlier stage, together with one or more other specialists; or they might be experts with narrower specialisms, whose responsibilities might be geographically more widely spread. They would be a *district handicap team*, in the sense referred to in the Court Report*, but with strong representation of the education service. (District handicap teams already in existence should be supplemented with membership from the education service.)

In addition to these teams assessing severely handicapped children or children with complex learning problems, there might be a need for regionally based teams of professionals to deal with the small minority of children with very rare or complex conditions. These regional teams should work at centres for handicapped children which should be set up in university hospitals. Again it is essential that the education service should be fully represented.

SE Forms and recording

When a child's special educational needs are assessed by a multi-professional team at Stage 4 or 5 the results must be carefully documented. To meet the child's needs as effectively as possible, an SE Form* should be filled in and sent to the education officer of the appropriate local education authority responsible for special education. The education officer might delegate the responsibility to a member of the *special education advisory and support service*.

Placement of each child would involve the advisory and support service of the local authority, in accordance with the evidence and conclusions of the multi-professional team

---

**Fit for the future*. The Committee on Child Health Services. Cmnd 6684 (HMSO 1976)

*In England and Wales, Form SE1 is intended for completion by a child's teacher, Form SE2 by the school doctor, Form SE3 by the educational psychologist, and Form SE4 is a summary and action sheet for completion by an experienced educational psychologist or advisor in special education. The use of the Forms is not at present mandatory. Scottish practice is on similar lines, though the sequence of the forms is different.

who assessed the child, together with a contribution from his parents. No placement would be made without the completed Form SE4. The Committee recognised that there was a danger that the more professionals there were involved in contributing to the completion of the SE Forms the more likely there were to be delays in placement. The Committee therefore suggested that the task of expediting the processing of the forms should be a main function of the 'named person' (mentioned above).

A new version of the SE Forms needs to be drawn up, with scope for contributions from the social as well as health and education services; parents also need to fill in a form – and be offered help in doing so – so that their information about their child's progress will be part of the evidence leading to placement.

The completed Form SE4 would form the basis on which the local education authority would judge whether or not a child should be recorded as requiring special educational provision. The record of the child's needs would be confidential, consisting of a file, to be kept in the local education authority's offices. It would comprise the completed Form SE4, containing a profile of the child's special needs and a recommendation for the provision of special help, as well as a separate note of how those needs were being met in practice, and the name of the person designated by the multi-professional assessment team to be the 'named person' for the child's parents.

Parents should have ready access to all these documents. They should also have the right of appeal to the Secretary of State against the decision by the local authority either to record their child, or not to do so. As the file would contain a statement of needs it would make it easy for parents to decide whether in their opinion their child's needs were actually being met.

Not all children who are recorded as requiring special educational provision would be educated in special schools. Many of the special provisions required are likely to be made available in at least some ordinary schools. But the criterion by which to judge whether a child should be recorded is whether he needs special arrangements which are not *normally* available in ordinary schools. Thus if a child's needs can be met only if he is taught in a small group it may be that in some ordinary schools special staffing arrangements could be made to render this possible; but such arrangements would not be thought of as part of the normal school provision.

The great advantage of this system of recording would be that if a child moved to another school it would be possible to ensure the continuity of the good arrangements which prevailed before the move. The new school might have a suitable unit for the particular child, or, alternatively a special school might be more suitable if an ordinary one could not make the necessary provision. Recording would be a way of ensuring that no child with significant difficulties was being overlooked as far as educational needs were concerned, once these had been assessed.

Finally, it is a necessary part of the Committee's recommendations about assessment that the progress of every child with special educational needs, whether he is recorded or not, should be carefully monitored and clearly noted. Parents should be entitled to seek a review of their child's progress at any time; and headteachers of schools, whether ordinary or special schools, should be responsible for initiating a review of progress annually. If a reassessment of the child's needs was thought necessary it could be carried out at any of the five stages already described. Reassessment would in any case be necessary two years before a young person with special needs was due to leave school, and should take into account his own and his parents' aspirations for and apprehensions about the future.

Continuum of provision

Such, then, are the Committee's proposals for the education of children with special needs from the time they are five until they are ready to leave school. Just as there is a continuum of educational needs, so there would be a continuum of special educational provision to meet these needs. There would be no sharp line between 'special' and 'ordinary' education, but within ordinary schools and special classes or units attached to them, and within special schools, children should receive the educational help they need in order to progress along the path towards the goals common to all education.

The training of teachers
But if this approach is to work in practice, not only must discovery, assessment and re-assessment be careful and professional, but teachers in ordinary and special schools and classes must be ready and able to recognise signs of special educational need, set in train the proper procedures of assessment at one of the five stages, and contribute their recorded observations to that assessment. The proposals of the Committee therefore laid a tremendous responsibility on teachers. This realisation led to the third of the Committee's list of equal top priorities, *namely the training of teachers*. No improvements in special educational provision can be achieved without certain essential and marked advances in teacher training.

Teachers will need to acquire a positive and optimistic attitude towards recognising children with special needs and securing help for them. They must take it for granted that they will work closely with parents and they will need to be ready to consult and work alongside other professionals concerned with the needs of children. Such a readiness can be ensured only through the content of training.

Teachers must be willing to accept the new wide concept of special educational need and must learn to expect that they may have up to five or six children in an ordinary class in need of temporary or permanent help. They must be aware that it is their job to take steps to see that children's needs are met, first and foremost by seeking skilled help. These considerations apply to all teachers, whatever the age of their pupils.

In addition, those teachers who have a defined responsibility for children with special educational needs should have considerable expertise and the confidence and status that go with it, if they are to work effectively. They should therefore be specially trained and able to collaborate effectively with medical and other professionals. Without this close working link the Committee's proposals will never be put into practice. In both these areas, the Committee made recommendations of the highest priority.

Special education element for all teachers

In the first place they recommended that *all courses of initial teacher training* – including postgraduate certificate courses – *should include a special education element*. The Committee recognised the practical difficulties of including this element in existing courses but was convinced that such an element is essential in all initial courses. It considered that when more children with special needs were being educated in ordinary schools, Section 10 of the 1976 Act – intended to be a great step forward for handicapped children – would be seen as a disaster for the children concerned unless their teachers were trained to help them or to seek help for them from appropriate sources.

It was not thought that this special education element should necessarily occupy a great many extra hours in the teacher training curriculum. In the first place, child development is already included in all courses. This subject could be so taught in future that teachers would learn to be on the alert to notice different patterns and rates of development in different children, and to recognise the effects of different common disabilities and other factors which influence development. In addition, teachers should become acquainted in the most general terms with the range of special educational provision available and the specialist advisory services. They should also be encouraged to view their relationships with parents as a partnership, without which special educational provision may fail. Teachers must be taught not only skills of observation but also skills of recording the progress and achievements of individual children.

Many of these things are changes of attitude or of interest rather than new subjects altogether; and though at first the attitudes may seem strange, and the concept of special educational need tiresome and intrusive, in time it will seem natural.

The Committee realised that it is no use insisting on the necessity for a special education element in all initial training if those teachers already in post have no chance to acquire the same assumptions, attitudes and skills. It would be forty years at least before all teachers would have taken a form of initial training which included this element. Therefore, short in-service courses for serving teachers which would cover the same ground as the proposed special education element should be set up immediately and be taken by the great majority of teachers within the next few years. This should be seen as necessary for the successful implementation of Section 10 of the 1976 Act. The courses would involve about a week's full-time study or its part-time equivalent. Where part-time, they should not be too widely spaced in time. The courses should be devised by the Education Departments in collaboration with Her Majesty's Inspectorate, local education authority representatives and the Open University and other academic bodies – *and the initiative should be taken at once*. The implementation of this proposal would be expensive; at least 200 additional full-time lecturers, or their part-time equivalents, would be needed if most serving teachers were to take the course within five years. *Nevertheless, if special educational provision is to be extended in ordinary schools and if such provision is not to be inadequate and inferior, such expense is necessary.*

Options in special education

Besides the special education element in every initial training course, it is also desirable that there should be a range of options open to teachers in training concerned with different aspects of special education. The Committee was not, however, much in favour of initial training specifically directed to the teaching of children with special needs, though it did not wish to see discontinued those courses already in existence in England and Wales with a strong bias towards the teaching of children with severe learning difficulties. The Committee's general view was that specialisation should come after initial training.

In-service training

In-service training, too, is at the very centre of the proposals for teacher training, both to give those teachers already in post the equivalent of the special education element in future initial training, and to supply courses leading to a specialist qualification. In principle the Committee held that all teachers with defined responsibilities for children with special educational needs, wherever they are receiving their education, should have an additional qualification in special eduaction, and so there should be a wide range of recognised qualifications obtainable at the end of a one year full-time course, or its part-time equivalent.

Moreover, all such qualifications would entitle a qualified teacher to extra payment under the terms of the Burnham Salaries document, suitably amended, and this extra payment should continue to be made after a teacher had reached the maximum of his salary scale whether teaching in an ordinary or a special school. There would therefore be a financial incentive for teachers to take these courses and qualify themselves.

The Committee proposed that in the long term, the possession of such a qualification should be made a requirement on all teachers with defined responsibility for children with special educational needs. Such a requirement could not be introduced immediately, but training facilities and local authority support for teachers to use them would need to be substantially increased with a view to such a requirement being introduced.

Furthermore, it was thought that there should be a range of extra, more specialist, courses for teachers wishing to specialise in different specific areas of handicap or learning difficulty. Such provision might well need to be established on a regional basis. There would need to be considerable development of the joint use of staff and of teaching materials by a number of colleges and departments, and the running of courses would be seen as an essential part of a regional network of facilities. The proposed new use of certain special schools as resource centres (see page 13 above) would be fundamental here. The schools would act as training bases for teachers and members of their staffs would be invited to contribute as visiting lecturers to courses in colleges and departments of education in all the different courses, and options within courses, which would exist there.

Further education teachers
With the hoped-for increase in opportunities for young

people with special needs to continue into further education it will be important that those who teach them should also have training in managing their problems. The initial training of all teachers in further education should include a special element – with a chance for those already teaching to make up this element through in-service short courses – and those who teach young people with special needs outside actual colleges of further education should also have access to the same range of training courses as their colleagues in the colleges.

Teachers with disabilities

The Committee held that there should be better opportunities for people with disabilities themselves to become teachers and to obtain teaching posts in both special and ordinary schools. At present there is a waste not only of talent but also of the particular contribution which teachers with disabilities can make in the field of education as a whole.

Attracting able teachers; and paying the costs

Two general points need to be made about these proposals. First, it is part of their aim that the career structure and the prospects for teachers of children with special needs should become more attractive. It is essential, if the recommendations of the Committee are to lead to the improvement of special education, that teachers of the highest calibre should be attracted into it, and that both their salaries and their prestige should be commensurate with their abilities. Secondly, putting these proposals into practice is going to be very expensive. For one thing, all the proposals will be frustrated unless local education authorities are willing to second teachers to study full-time and to support those who wish to study part-time. Authorities must be encouraged to do this. However it is certain that they will not do it, at least on the scale required, if they have to include the costs in the calculation of relevant expenditure for rate support grant purposes.

Most of the Committee believed that the only realistic way of ensuring the release of teachers would be through the payment of specifically earmarked government grants to cover the whole cost, unpopular though this might be with local authorities. Such a suggestion would never have been made if the Committee had not seen that all their proposals for the improvement of educational provision for children with special needs turned on the supply of properly trained teachers, confident of their ability to help children, in whatever setting, respected by their colleagues, both in the teaching profession and other crucially related professions, and enjoying also the confidence and respect of parents.

Besides the question of releasing teachers to be trained there is also the question of providing extra lecturers to train them. In this respect, however, though expenditure will inevitably be involved, the time is favourable: teacher training has contracted and lecturers, teachers and accommodation are all available. The present favourable opportunity should be seized.

Three priorities
These, then, were the three equal priorities which the Committee put forward: education of children with special needs before the age of five, with no age limit; education and increased opportunities for young people over the age of sixteen; and a new programme of teacher training.

Advisory and support service
There is a further condition upon which the implementation of the Committee's recommendations depends and that is the setting up, within each local authority, of an *advisory and support service for special education.* Much very valuable work is already being carried out by advisers in special and remedial education, by advisory and peripatetic remedial teachers working with children with different disabilities and by home visiting teachers working mainly with young children. All the same, these special services are at present often somewhat fragmented, with different teachers working to different administrative officers and a lack of contact between those concerned with the various arrangements for education elsewhere than at school. For effective use of all this expertise and in the new framework of education for children with special needs it is essential that the provision of advice and support, both to schools and parents, should be coordinated, restructured and if

necessary increased, *to provide a unified and coherent service.*

This is not to suggest a whole new bureaucracy of advisers and others, set above the actual teachers. The support service proposed would consist mainly of existing advisers and advisory teachers, reinforced by a number of practising teachers who could either spend part of their time in the classroom or could be seconded to the service for a limited period. If the school population continues to decrease and if the number of children in special schools contracts there should also be scope for the redeployment of senior and experienced teachers in special schools as full or part-time members of the service.

The aims of the service should be first, to raise and maintain the standards of special education generally; and, secondly, to help with the teaching of individual children. In the first capacity, members of the service should be deeply involved in the running of in-service and other courses for teachers, contributing to the courses themselves and arranging for other professionals concerned with children with special needs to take part. In their second capacity, they should be involved in the assessment of the needs of individual children at the various stages described earlier and be responsible for the SE forms procedure and for monitoring and developing school-based assessment. The development of special schools as resource centres would also be a part of their function (and some of the senior staff of special schools would normally be members of the service).

The service should also be the source of advice to the local education authority about placement, with the best interest of the individual child, rather than consideration of administrative convenience, as the criterion. Its members would also be a source of help and guidance to parents. In the case of children recorded as requiring special educational provision a member of the service might well be nominated by the assessment team as the 'named person' for their parents. In all these ways, and doubtless in others, the special education advisory and support service would operate as the force by means of which the new concept of special education would be accepted and prove its effectiveness and worth in practice.

The Committee thought that the establishment of such a service in every local education authority should begin at once: the establishment of a structure would cost very little, and, within the structure, existing staff could be employed. Over a period of years the service could be developed and improved, as it became clearer where the most urgent needs lay. Meanwhile, members of the service should themselves have training, at every level.

The Committee proposed that a Special Education Staff College should be set up (not necessarily with a geographical location) to arrange for courses and seminars and conferences for those working in special education at a senior level, where ideas could be discussed and expertise disseminated. In this way, and through the advisory and support services themselves, the quality of education for children with special needs and its distribution over the whole country could be steadily improved.

Cooperation

From everything that has been said so far it will be plain that the education of children with special needs cannot be thought of in isolation. It is not a neat packet which can be offered to those who need it, in a single context, or at any precisely defined age. Education must start before school and go on after school. It must be available at home, in hospital, in community homes and in training centres just as much as in schools or colleges. And if this is to be a reality, not merely a pious hope, there is need for intense and serious cooperation between those who are primarily educationists and those who do not normally think of themselves in this light. Parents, it cannot be too often stressed, must, wherever possible, be treated as equal partners in the educational enterprise, and there must be close collaboration between the health and the social services. The feeling that teachers are interested in academic learning, while doctors and social workers are interested in therapy or caring, must be dispelled. All the professions must somehow learn to come to a fuller understanding of the contribution of the others.

Teachers are not, of course, the only people employed in the education service who will be involved. There are educational psychologists, careers officers, education welfare officers, nursery nurses, child care staff and ancillary workers of various kinds, all of whom make important contributions to the service of children with special needs.

In the health service perhaps the most important contributors are school doctors and nurses. The Committee believes that there *should be a named doctor and nurse (with appropriate experience and skills) for every school*, whether a special or an ordinary school, to develop a close and mutually trusting relationship between the education and health professionals.

Similarly, social workers, who sometimes seem to work in isolation from their colleagues in the education service, need to be given, as part of their training, an understanding of the educational services available to children and parents who will come into their care, so that it is taken for granted that there will be liaison between the two services.

There is still a long way to go on the thorny track of coordinating all the different contributing services but it is important for local authorities to set up, under the auspices of Joint Consultative Committees, working groups to review the whole range of provision of services for children and young people up to the age of 25, in order jointly to make good any deficiencies they find.

Moreover, regional conferences for special education, which already exist in England and Wales, should extend their functions to include consideration of the findings of such working groups. Membership of these regional conferences should include, besides local education authority members and officers, representatives of employment, health and social services, employers' and employees' organisations and teachers responsible for children with special educational needs. Only by means of such deliberate arrangements will the problems of cooperation in general, and specific problems such as those which arise from considerations of confidentiality between professions, begin to be solved. A more ambitious service of special education would compound and magnify the difficulties of cooperation unless positive and deliberate steps are taken locally to break the barriers down.

Voluntary organisations

Two further areas were of particular concern to the Committee: the place of voluntary organisations and the need for increased research. It saw a continuing important place for *voluntary organisations* in the improvement of education of children with special needs. They should continue to cooperate with local authorities in the provision of services and in spreading to parents of children with special needs information about the provision available. There will always be some people in need of help who will seek it, if at all, only from those who are outside the statutory providing establishment. And it is extremely desirable that there should be independent and deeply committed organisations to act as pressure groups, whether locally or nationally, to improve provision for those whose cause they have taken up: this has traditionally been the function of voluntary organisations, and it must continue.

Research and the curriculum

The Committee was also anxious to see *increased research* into the needs of children with disabilities and significant difficulties of various kinds. Above all, the research should be coordinated and its results properly disseminated and translated into practice. There should be at least one university department of special education in every region of the country and priority should be given in universities and polytechnics to the establishment of senior posts in this field. Some of these posts should be linked to part-time work with children, not only in medicine but in psychology and education as well. Lecturers in special education in colleges should have time for research, and educational psychologists should also be involved. Those special schools which become resource centres should provide opportunities for members of different professions to work together on research projects — this would include practising teachers. The centres would be valuable store-houses of material.

In order that research be carried out in fields where most needed, and to minimise duplication of work, the Committee recommended the establishment of a *Special Education Research Group*, with responsibility for indicating priorities and identifying programmes to be initiated. It should have a budget large enough to support one or two projects at any given time, and several smaller ones.

One of the main areas of research will be the curriculum. Research and development are closely interlinked. The Committee held that curriculum development in special education should arise naturally from the work of schools, whether special schools or ordinary schools, and that teachers should be looked to and encouraged to see themselves as a source of expertise. The Committee argued that resources should be made available to the Schools Council, to the Consultative Committee on the Curriculum in Scotland and to local teachers' centres so that curriculum projects could be translated into forms useful to special schools, units and classes. Each kind of educational difficulty and special need would have its own curricular requirements. The aim would be to ensure that children with special needs had access to the general curriculum so far as possible. They, like all children, need to understand the world they live in and to have opportunities to develop their imaginative powers, for example in art and music. The Committee therefore emphasised the importance of developing new ways of making the common curriculum available to children with special needs.

For the research and curriculum developments to be fruitful in terms of improved practice and expertise, local education authorities would need to see that their teachers centres were fully used, and perhaps a centre set up in which all research and in-service training for teachers of children with special needs were based. At national level, the establishment of the Special Education Staff College would ensure the dissemination of new knowledge among administrators and senior advisers.

Summing up
Such were the Committee's main conclusions. It proposed a new conceptual framework, within which special educational provision should be made. This entails a continuum of special educational need rather than discreet categories of handicap. It embraces children with significant learning difficulties and emotional or behavioural disorders, as well as those with disabilities of

mind or body; it takes in the present concept of remedial, as well as special, education, and is not committed to any one place in which education should be given. Within such a framework all the key proposals for the discovery, assessment and recording of special educational needs, the duties of local education authorities and the involvement of parents were set. This conceptual framework should be reflected in the legislation which it is hoped might be introduced without delay.

There was much that the Committee thought could be done meanwhile. In the first place, if Section 10 of the 1976 Education Act is to come into force, a programme of teacher training needs to be initiated straightaway. Local education authorities must have a coherent plan, according to which services for all children with special educational needs can be provided. These things need not wait for legislation; a start can be made at once.

As far as resources went, it was not possible for the Committee to be precise in costing its various recommendations. It assumed that finance would be forthcoming to provide the extra resources necessary for the implementation of Section 10. Moreover there are some respects in which the report has come at a favourable time. School rolls are falling, and both buildings and teachers are becoming available. It was thought that a good deal of the Committee's recommendations could be financed from existing budgets. Where the Committee believed that extra resources would be urgently needed it has said so.

The Committee summed up its report in the following words:
> Organisational changes and additional resources will not be sufficient in themselves to achieve our aims. They must be accompanied by changes in attitudes. Special education must be seen as a form of educational activity no less important, no less demanding and no less rewarding than any other, and teachers, administrators and other professionals engaged in it must have the same commitment to children with special needs as they have to other children. Nor will it be enough if these changes in attitude are confined to people engaged in special education. Changes in attitude are also necessary on the part of the public at large. There must be a general

acceptance of the idea that special education involves as much skill and professional expertise as any other form of education and that in human terms the returns on resources invested in it are just as great.

It is hoped that all those who read and consider the conclusions of the Committee will both share and disseminate the new approach themselves.

Printed in the UK for HMSO by Hobbs the Printers of Southampton
(2792) Dd738222 C20 10/85 G3379